EVERYTHING PROGRESSIVES AND CONSERVATIVES KNOW ABOUT CHRISTIANITY

A Moderate Perspective
Franklyn James

Everything Progressives and Conservatives Know about Christianity:
A Moderate Perspective
© 2025 Franklyn James

All rights reserved. No part of this publication may be reproduced, stored in a retrieval system, or transmitted in any form or by any means, electronic, mechanical, photocopying, recording, or otherwise, without prior written permission of the publisher, except for brief quotations in reviews, critical articles, or scholarly works.

Scripture quotations, where included, are from the *New Revised Standard Version Bible, Updated Edition,* © 2021 National Council of Churches of Christ in the USA. Used by permission. All rights reserved worldwide.

Published by Kairos House Press

First Edition

Paperback ISBN: 979-8-9987699-8-6
eBook ISBN: 979-8-9987699-9-3

The Christian ideal has not been tried and found wanting. It has been found difficult; and left untried.

G. K. Chesterton,
What's Wrong with the World (1910)

CONTENTS

Introduction vii

1	The Gospel According to Soundbites	1
2	When Christ Becomes a Campaign Slogan	15
3	Strange Things We've Heard in the Name of Christ	29
4	God Said What?!	43
5	The Gospel of Left and Right: The Four Horsemen of the Culture War	57
6	Rome Fell. Christianity Did Not.	71
7	The Idol of Certainty	85
8	Silence: The Gospel's Dangerous Gift or Deadly Curse	99
9	A Faith Too Wild to Cage	113

Bibliography 127
Reader's Guide: Questions for Reflection 135
About the Author 139

INTRODUCTION

Over the last 11 months, the political climate has mirrored that of first-century Rome, when the empire was gasping under the weight of its own contradictions, with military triumphs abroad masking decay at home, wealth and spectacle distracting from inequality, and populist rhetoric serving as the stage for power struggles. It was in that world, amid the collapse of imperial certainty, that Christianity was born..

The early church emerged not from the center of an empire but from its edges: a backwater province, a crucified Messiah, a collection of house gatherings without armies, marble halls, or party platforms. And yet, what began as fragile communities of faith evolved into the largest religious movement in human history. This irony is not lost on us today. As political parties and ideologues across the globe once again wield Christianity like a sword or a shield to prove their cause, disprove their enemies, or baptize their biases, we are reminded of the strange birthright of this faith: it was never meant to be a tool of power, but it has always been vulnerable to those who would use it as one.

In our present age, Christianity is a prop in debates that often have little to do with the gospel itself. Progressives cite Jesus as the first social revolutionary, the champion of inclusion, the preacher of radical love. Conservatives invoke Him as guardian of family values, defender of order, and guarantor of absolute truth. Both sides quote selectively. Both sides canonize their agendas. And both sides, despite their differences, mirror each other in their certainty that Christ belongs squarely in their camp. The one thing they share, though they rarely admit, is an inability to imagine a Christianity that critiques their positions rather than endorses them. *But what of those who are weary of the shouting? What of the curious, the moderate, the faithful who sense that Christianity is deeper than partisanship and truer than any ideology? This book is written with you in mind.*

We live in unprecedented times. Public figures are assassinated or silenced through violence and censorship. Political leaders face repeated attempts on their lives, as rage replaces reason, dialogue is abandoned, and honest debate is treated as taboo. Religion is drawn into the struggle, and in the Western world Christianity has become the cannon of the culture wars. Yet it is not only the West. Across the globe, other faiths and traditions face the same temptation: to turn the sacred into a weapon of identity and power. This begs the question: when people enlist faith for their causes, what do we really know about the faith they invoke and claim to uphold?

The church's history tells us this much: the gospel resists capture, and every empire that sought to claim it was the one that crumbled. When Rome fell, Christianity did not. When emperors remade Christ into an imperial mascot, martyrs and mystics remembered another way. When ideologues twisted doctrine to their advantage, voices from deserts and councils insisted that faith could not be reduced to slogans. The story of the church is one of survival not because it aligned with the winning side, but because, time and again, it endured long after every empire, party, and ideology collapsed.

This book is a needed provocation. You will open its pages expecting arguments, footnotes, and polemics. Instead, you will find wisdom in its margins for prophetic imagination. The insight hidden between the pages is the most honest representation of what Progressives and Conservatives, as movements of our age, truly know about Christianity. Faith cannot be contained by their talking points, nor the gospel reduced to their sound bites. These pages stand as a mirror, daring you to consider whether you have mistaken Christianity for ideology, or Christ for a campaign surrogate.

The satire hides a serious purpose. For centuries, scholars have produced libraries of work on the origins of the church, the texture of its scriptures, the voices of its Fathers and Mothers, the archaeology of its rituals, and the anthropology of its growth. This introduction includes both an extensive bibliography and a reader's guide. The guide is not a study aid with ready-made answers; it is a set of questions for reflection. These questions are written for all readers: Christians, skeptics, seekers, politicians, people of other faiths, and those who claim no faith at all.

The aim is not to argue anyone into belief but to invite honest reflection on how Christianity has shaped, troubled, or intersected with the world each reader knows. Knowledge exists. Wisdom has been pursued. Thoughtful, brilliant, and even saintly women and men have wrestled with Christianity in all its complexity. They did not flatten it into talking points. They did not weaponize it into hashtags. They recognized that faith could be questioned, doubted, deepened, and lived, but never monopolized.

If this book succeeds, it will not be because of what you read here but because of what you will not find in the pages that follow. Their spaciousness is a place for your imagination, your critique, and perhaps your confession. For when all the noise is stripped away, when the Progressives and Conservatives stop shouting across the aisle, what remains is the uncomfortable silence of a gospel that refuses to be co-opted.

Like Rome before it, every ideology eventually crumbles. Christianity has survived not because it was the perfect partner of empire or democracy, but because, in its essence, it does not belong to any of them. It is older than liberalism, deeper than conservatism, and larger than any moderate attempt to referee the fight. Its true power is not in political capture but in the stubborn witness of a crucified Messiah and the communities that dare to live as though love is stronger than death.

So here, at the threshold of yet another cultural collapse, you hold in your hands a paradox: a book with no book, an argument with no words, a library distilled into silence. May these pages trouble you. May the bibliography humble you. And may the moderate perspective remind you that Christianity is not the servant of ideology, but the haunting voice that judges them all.

CHAPTER 1

THE GOSPEL ACCORDING TO SOUNDBITES

Everything Progressives and Conservatives Know about Christianity

The Gospel According to Soundbites

The Gospel According to Soundbites

Everything Progressives and Conservatives Know about Christianity

The Gospel According to Soundbites

The Gospel According to Soundbites

The Gospel According to Soundbites

The Gospel According to Soundbites

CHAPTER 2

WHEN CHRIST BECOMES A CAMPAIGN SLOGAN

When Christ Becomes a Campaign Slogan

When Christ Becomes a Campaign Slogan

When Christ Becomes a Campaign Slogan

When Christ Becomes a Campaign Slogan

When Christ Becomes a Campaign Slogan

When Christ Becomes a Campaign Slogan

CHAPTER 3

STRANGE THINGS WE'VE HEARD IN THE NAME OF CHRIST

Strange Things We've Heard in the Name of Christ

Strange Things We've Heard in the Name of Christ

CHAPTER 4

GOD SAID WHAT?!

God Said What?!

CHAPTER 5

THE GOSPEL OF LEFT AND RIGHT: THE FOUR HORSEMEN OF THE CULTURE WAR

The Gospel of Left and Right: The Four Horsemen of the Culture War

The Gospel of Left and Right: The Four Horsemen of the Culture War

The Gospel of Left and Right: The Four Horsemen of the Culture War

The Gospel of Left and Right: The Four Horsemen of the Culture War

CHAPTER 6

ROME FELL. CHRISTIANITY DID NOT.

Rome Fell. Christianity Did Not.

Rome Fell. Christianity Did Not.

Rome Fell. Christianity Did Not.

Rome Fell. Christianity Did Not.

Rome Fell. Christianity Did Not.

Rome Fell. Christianity Did Not.

CHAPTER 7

THE IDOL OF CERTAINTY

The Idol of Certainty

The Idol of Certainty

The Idol of Certainty

The Idol of Certainty

The Idol of Certainty

CHAPTER 8

SILENCE: THE GOSPEL'S DANGEROUS GIFT OR DEADLY CURSE

CHAPTER 9

A FAITH TOO WILD TO CAGE

A Faith Too Wild to Cage

A Faith Too Wild to Cage

A Faith Too Wild to Cage

A Faith Too Wild to Cage

A Faith Too Wild to Cage

A Faith Too Wild to Cage

BIBLIOGRAPHY

Archaeology & Historical Context

Benjamin, Don C. 2010. *Stones and Stories: An Introduction to Archaeology and the Bible*. Minneapolis: Fortress Press.

Cline, Eric H. 2009. *Biblical Archaeology: A Very Short Introduction*. Oxford: Oxford University Press.

Currid, John D. 2020. *The Case for Biblical Archaeology: Uncovering the Historical Record of God's Old Testament People*. Wheaton: Crossway.

Dever, William G. 2003. *Who Were the Early Israelites and Where Did They Come From?* Grand Rapids, MI: William B. Eerdmans Publishing Company.

Finkelstein, Israel, and Neil Asher Silberman. 2001. *The Bible Unearthed: Archaeology's New Vision of Ancient Israel and the Origin of Its Sacred Texts*. New York: Free Press.

Freund, Richard A. 2009. *Digging Through the Bible: Modern Archaeology and the Ancient Bible*. New York: HarperOne.

Frend, William H. C. 1996. *The Archaeology of Early Christianity: A History*. Minneapolis: Fortress Press.

Gibson, Shimon. 2009. *The Final Days of Jesus: The Archaeological Evidence*. New York: HarperOne.

Harris, Roberta L. 2003. *The World of the Bible*. New York: Thames & Hudson.

Kitchen, Kenneth A. 2003. *On the Reliability of the Old Testament*. Grand Rapids, MI: William B. Eerdmans Publishing Company.

Commentaries

Anchor Yale Bible Commentary (AYBC). 1964–. *Anchor Yale Bible Commentary*. New Haven: Yale University Press.

Word Biblical Commentary (WBC). 1977–. *Word Biblical Commentary*. Grand Rapids, MI: Zondervan Academic.

New International Commentary on the New Testament (NICNT). 1953–. *New International Commentary on the New Testament*. Grand Rapids, MI: Eerdmans.

New International Commentary on the Old Testament (NICOT). 1965–. *New International Commentary on the Old Testament*. Grand Rapids, MI: Eerdmans.

Hermeneia Commentary Series. 1971–. *Hermeneia: A Critical and Historical Commentary on the Bible*. Minneapolis: Fortress Press.

New Interpreter's Bible (NIB). 1994–. *The New Interpreter's Bible*. 12 vols. Nashville: Abingdon Press.

The New Interpreter's Bible Commentary (NIBC). 2015. *The New Interpreter's Bible Commentary*. 1 vol. Edited by Leander E. Keck. Nashville: Abingdon Press.

The New Oxford Annotated Bible (NOAB). 1962–2018. *The New Oxford Annotated Bible with the Apocrypha*. Various eds. New York: Oxford University Press.

Dictionaries, Encyclopedias & Reference

Bromiley, Geoffrey W., ed. 1979–1988. *International Standard Bible Encyclopedia.* 4 vols. Grand Rapids, MI: William B. Eerdmans Publishing Company.

Cross, F. L., and E. A. Livingstone, eds. 2005. *The Oxford Dictionary of the Christian Church.* Oxford: Oxford University Press.

Elwell, Walter A., ed. 2001. *Evangelical Dictionary of Theology.* Grand Rapids: Baker Academic.

Evans, Craig A., and Stanley E. Porter, eds. 2000. *Dictionary of New Testament Background.* Downers Grove, IL: InterVarsity Press.

Freedman, David Noel, ed. 1992. *Anchor Bible Dictionary.* 6 vols. New York: Doubleday.

González, Justo L. 2010. *The Story of Christianity.* 2 vols. New York: HarperOne.

Kelly, Joseph F. 2009. *The Concise Dictionary of Early Christianity.* Collegeville, MN: Liturgical Press.

Latourette, Kenneth Scott. 1975. *A History of Christianity.* Rev. ed. New York: Harper & Row.

McGrath, Alister E. 2016. *Christian Theology: An Introduction.* 6th ed. Hoboken, NJ: Wiley-Blackwell.

Wace, Henry, ed. 1994. *A Dictionary of Christian Biography and Literature to the End of the Sixth Century A.D.* Peabody, MA: Hendrickson.

Anthropology & Cultural Context

Aune, David E. 1987. *The New Testament in Its Literary Environment*. Philadelphia: Westminster John Knox.

Geertz, Clifford. 1973. *The Interpretation of Cultures*. New York: Basic Books.

Kugel, James, and Rowan Greer. 1986. *Early Biblical Interpretation*. Philadelphia: Westminster John Knox Press.

Malherbe, Abraham J. 1986. *Moral Exhortation: A Greco-Roman Sourcebook*. Philadelphia: Westminster John Knox.

Meeks, Wayne A. 1986. *The Moral World of the First Christians*. Philadelphia: Westminster John Knox.

Stowers, Stanley. 1986. *Letter Writing in Greco-Roman Antiquity*. Philadelphia: Westminster John Knox.

Early Christian Voices and Primary Texts

Augustine of Hippo. 2004. *The City of God*. Translated by Henry Bettenson. London: Penguin Classics.

Athanasius. 2011. *On the Incarnation*. Translated and edited by John Behr. Popular Patristics Series 44a. Crestwood, NY: St. Vladimir's Seminary Press.

Clement of Alexandria. 1919. *Exhortation to the Greeks. The Rich Man's Salvation. To the Newly Baptized*. Translated by G. W. Butterworth. Loeb Classical Library. Cambridge, MA: Harvard University Press; London: William Heinemann.

Cyprian of Carthage. 1957. *The Lapsed: The Unity of the Catholic Church.* Translated and annotated by Maurice Bévenot, SJ. Ancient Christian Writers 25. Westminster, MD: The Newman Press; London: Longmans, Green & Co.

Eusebius of Caesarea. 1998. *Ecclesiastical History: Complete and Unabridged.* Translated by C. F. Cruse. Peabody, MA: Hendrickson.

Gregory of Nyssa. 1916. *The Life of St. Macrina.* Translated by W. K. Lowther Clarke. Early Church Classics. London: Society for Promoting Christian Knowledge.

Irenaeus of Lyons. 1992–. *Against the Heresies.* 5 vols. Translated and annotated by Dominic J. Unger, revised by John J. Dillon. Ancient Christian Writers 55–64. Mahwah, NJ: Newman Press.

Heffernan, Thomas J., trans. 2012. *The Passion of Perpetua and Felicity.* Oxford: Oxford University Press.

Josephus, Flavius. 1980. *The Works of Josephus: Complete and Unabridged, New Updated Edition.* Translated by William Whiston. Peabody, MA: Hendrickson Publishers.

Tertullian and Minucius Felix. 1931. *Apology. De Spectaculis. Minucius Felix : Octavius.* Translated by T. R. Glover and Gerald H. Rendall. Loeb Classical Library 250. Cambridge, MA: Harvard University Press.

Ward, Benedicta, trans. 1975. *The Sayings of the Desert Fathers: The Alphabetical Collection.* Kalamazoo, MI: Cistercian Publications.

Contemporary Scholarly Works

Barr, Beth Allison. 2021. *The Making of Biblical Womanhood: How the Subjugation of Women Became Gospel Truth.* Grand Rapids, MI: Brazos Press.

Billings, J. Todd. 2020. *The End of the Christian Life: How Embracing Our Mortality Frees Us to Truly Live.* Grand Rapids, MI: Brazos Press.

Childers, Alisa. 2020. *Another Gospel? A Lifelong Christian Seeks Truth in Response to Progressive Christianity.* Eugene, OR: Harvest House Publishers.

Douglas, Kelly Brown. 2015. *Stand Your Ground: Black Bodies and the Justice of God.* Maryknoll, NY: Orbis Books.

Du Mez, Kristin Kobes. 2020. *Jesus and John Wayne: How White Evangelicals Corrupted a Faith and Fractured a Nation.* New York: Liveright Publishing.

Engel, Connie. 2021. *The Progressive Church: A Dangerous Movement That Must Be Stopped.* Self-published.

Hart, David Bentley. 2019. *That All Shall Be Saved: Heaven, Hell, and Universal Salvation.* New Haven: Yale University Press.

Jensen, Dan. 2017. *A False Kind of Christianity: A Conservative Evangelical Refutation of Progressive Christianity.* Bloomington, IN: Westbow Press.

Luhrmann, T. M. 2020. *How God Becomes Real: Kindling the Presence of Invisible Others.* Princeton, NJ: Princeton University Press.

McCaulley, Esau. 2020. *Reading While Black: African American Biblical Interpretation as an Exercise in Hope.* Downers Grove, IL: IVP Academic.

Rutledge, Fleming. 2015. *The Crucifixion: Understanding the Death of Jesus Christ.* Grand Rapids, MI: Eerdmans.

Taylor, Charles. 2007. *A Secular Age.* Cambridge, MA: Belknap Press of Harvard University Press.

Trueman, Carl R. 2020. *The Rise and Triumph of the Modern Self: Cultural Amnesia, Expressive Individualism, and the Road to Sexual Revolution.* Wheaton, IL: Crossway.

Volf, Miroslav, and Ryan McAnnally-Linz. 2016. *Public Faith in Action: How to Think Carefully, Engage Wisely, and Vote with Integrity.* Grand Rapids, MI: Brazos Press.

READER'S GUIDE: QUESTIONS FOR REFLECTION

These questions are not only for Christians but for all readers: atheists, agnostics, spiritual seekers, politicians, people of other faiths, and those who claim no faith at all, the nones. The purpose is not to argue you into belief, but to invite you into honest reflection on how Christianity has shaped, troubled, or intersected with your world.

Your Lens

I. What assumptions, doubts, or experiences did you bring to this book?

II. How has Christianity touched or troubled your life, whether through family, culture, politics, or history?

Faith and Ideology

I. Where have you seen religion, Christianity or otherwise, turned into an instrument of ideology, power, or identity politics?

II. In your own worldview, how do you guard against slogans replacing substance?

The Public Square

    I. If you are a politician, how has Christianity been used in the political arena, you know?

    II. If you are a citizen, what role do you believe faith traditions should or should not play in shaping public life?

Silence and Space

    I. What do you notice in the "silence" of this book?

    II. Does space for imagination or critique feel freeing, frustrating, or unsettling to you? Why?

Beyond Christianity

    I. For people of other faiths or none: What parallels do you see between how Christianity is co-opted and how different traditions or secular ideals get politicized?

    II. What wisdom from your own background might contribute to a more humane and just dialogue?

Living with Critique

    I. How might you imagine a worldview, religious or secular, that critiques your own biases rather than endorses them?

    II. What practices, personal, communal, or political, help you keep humility alive?

    III. Which voices in the bibliography invite you to explore further?

ABOUT THE AUTHOR

Franklyn James is a Jamaican-born Canadian theologian, educator, and storyteller. With a deep commitment to justice, spiritual formation, and inclusive education, his work weaves history, mysticism, lived experience, and prophetic imagination into layered reflections on faith, power, and the human condition.

Franklyn's writing often speaks to the margins and the mystics, exploring themes such as identity, grief, intimacy, and resilience. As a critical thinker and compassionate provocateur, he challenges dominant narratives while inviting readers to sit with discomfort, beauty, and possibility.

His published works include *Tones of Transition*, *The Body in Narrative*, *The Little Things We Take for Granted*, *Shards of Longing*, and *Death: The Epithet of Excellence*. With *Everything Progressives and Conservatives Know about Christianity: A Moderate Perspective*, he turns to satire and space, offering readers a margin for wisdom, imagination, and critique.

www.ingramcontent.com/pod-product-compliance
Lightning Source LLC
Chambersburg PA
CBHW070631030426
42337CB00020B/3985